First World War
and Army of Occupation
War Diary
France, Belgium and Germany

50 DIVISION
Divisional Troops
Divisional Cyclist Company
16 April 1915 - 31 May 1916

WO95/2817/2

The Naval & Military Press Ltd
www.nmarchive.com
Published in association with The National Archives

Published by

The Naval & Military Press Ltd

Unit 10 Ridgewood Industrial Park,

Uckfield, East Sussex,

TN22 5QE England

Tel: +44 (0) 1825 749494

www.naval-military-press.com

www.nmarchive.com

This diary has been reprinted in facsimile from the original. Any imperfections are inevitably reproduced and the quality may fall short of modern type and cartographic standards.

© **Crown Copyright**
Images reproduced by permission of The National Archives, London, England, 2015.

Contents

Document type	Place/Title	Date From	Date To
Heading	WO95/2817-2		
Heading	50th Division Divl Cyclist Coy. Apr 1915-May 1916		
Miscellaneous	Cyclist Coy Vol 5		
Heading	Cyclist Co. 50th Div. 10 Apr to 31 Dec Vol I		
War Diary	Newcastle On Tyne	16/04/1915	20/04/1915
War Diary	Steenvoorde	15/05/1915	18/05/1915
War Diary	C Camp	18/05/1915	18/05/1915
War Diary	Brandhoek	19/05/1915	22/05/1915
War Diary	G.H.Q. Line In I.16a And I 16b (Sheet 28)	24/05/1915	23/06/1915
War Diary	Farm In G.26.a. (Sheet 28)	04/06/1915	23/06/1915
War Diary	St. Jans Capel	24/06/1915	19/07/1915
War Diary	Armentieres	19/07/1915	31/07/1915
War Diary	St. Jans Capel	06/07/1915	17/07/1915
War Diary	Armentieres	13/08/1915	12/11/1915
War Diary	Merris	12/11/1915	30/11/1915
War Diary	Armentieres	18/11/1915	18/11/1915
War Diary	Merris	01/12/1915	16/12/1915
War Diary	Wippenhoek	16/12/1915	31/12/1915
Heading	50th Division Cyclist Coy Jun Vol II		
War Diary	Wippenhoek	01/01/1916	31/03/1916
War Diary	Westoutre	01/04/1916	25/04/1916
War Diary	Fletre	25/04/1916	30/04/1916
War Diary	Westoutre	06/04/1916	06/04/1916
War Diary	Fletre	01/05/1916	21/05/1916
War Diary	Kemmel	22/05/1916	31/05/1916

6/28/17

(6/28/16)

6/28/17

(6/28/16)

50TH DIVISION

DIVL CYCLIST COY.

APR 1915-MAY 1916.

50

Cyclist Coy

Vol III 5

Cyrian Co. 56th In.

10 apr to 31 Dec

Vol I

WAR DIARY of 50th (North'n) Divisional Cyclist Company

or INTELLIGENCE SUMMARY.

Army Form C. 2118.

Re. MAPS 40,000

Hour, Date, Place	Summary of Events and Information	Remarks and references to Appendices
April 16th/4/15 Newcastle-on-Tyne	Left Benton Hall, Newcastle-on-Tyne, and proceed to Southampton. Strength of Company 8 Officers, 142 Other Ranks attached 2 R.A.M.C. 2 A.S.C. Transport of Company — 1 G.S. wagon (supplies) 1 G.S. wagon (baggage) 1 G.S. limber S.A.A. cart 1 heavy draught and 2 light draught horses	
7.30 P.M. 17/4/15	at Southampton on the paddle steamer La Marguerite	
4.0 A.M. 18/4/15	Sailed from SOUTHAMPTON	
12 (midnight) 18/4/15	Disembarked at HAVRE	
9.30 P.M. 19/4/15	Entrained at HAVRE	
8.0 A.M. 20/4/15	Detrained at HAZEBROUCK and spent the night in the Asylum. Left HAZEBROUCK and rode to STEENVOORDE where the Company was billeted until the 15th of May	
19/4/15 to 15/5/15	Work done by the Company during this period. Road Traffic control, Police control at POPERINGHE, Searching for ammunition and stores in the farms which had been used as billets by the troops. Patrolling roads in the district, and bringing	A. Nypaerd left O.C. 50th Div. Cyclist Coy

Army Form C. 2118.

WAR DIARY of 50th (North'n) Divisional Signal Company
or
INTELLIGENCE SUMMARY
(Erase heading not required.)

RE MAPS 1/40,000

Hour, Date, Place	Summary of Events and Information	Remarks and references to Appendices
5.30 P.M. May 15 1915 STEENVOORDE	in all stragglers, finding beds for Divisional H.Q.; Signal Training. Received orders to move to C Camp, BRIELEN, N.E. of VLAMERTINGHE and arrived there at 11.0 P.M. on the same night, and received orders that the Company was to work under the orders of the Cavalry Corps.	
4.0 P.M. May 16th to 4.0 A.M. May 18th C Camp	Bombarded at intervals. Total damage 1 Bay Mare 1 horse wounded and three others damaged.	
4.0 A.M. May 18th C Camp	Received orders from the 3 Cavalry Corps to move into billets in BRANDHOEK	
May 19th BRANDHOEK	The Company found working party for the R.E. who laid a truck to connect up two advanced parts of the front line	
May 22nd BRANDHOEK	The Company was ordered onto the G.H.Q. Line in I.16.a. and I.16.b. (sheet 28) as a working party and garrison.	
2.0 A.M. May 24th G.H.Q. Line in I.16.a. and I.16.b. (sheet 28)	The enemy started a very heavy artillery bombardment which lasted until 8.0 P.M. the same day. At dawn on 24 May the enemy began a gas attack followed by an infantry attack. The Company passed on this day:-	A M Gracie Capt
	LIEUT. J.L. REID } wounded 2nd LIEUT. G.O. HARPER } wounded	O.C. 50 Div Signal Coy

WAR DIARY of 50th (North'd) Divisional Cyclist Company

or

INTELLIGENCE SUMMARY.

Army Form C. 2118.

RE. MAPS. 1/40,000

Hour, Date, Place	Summary of Events and Information	Remarks and references to Appendices
May 19th to May 28th	Casualties of May 24th continued:— 4 Other Ranks killed. 18 Other Ranks wounded. During this time the Company supplied parties to look after Refugees 7 to 14 over the YSER CANAL WEST of YPRES, with orders to direct any stampeded ones to the bridges & ensure orders to the bridges by ensure	
9.0 A.M. May 25th	Coy. H.Q. The Company was asked to return from the G.H.Q line to A Camp, just South of VLAMERTINGHE on A Camp H.Qrs. (Sheet 28)	
May 25th to May 31st	The Company rested in A Camp H.Qrs. (Sheet 28)	

AMyracel
Capt. O.C.
50th Div. Cyclist Coy.

AMyracel Capt. O.C.
50 Div. Cyclist Coy.

WAR DIARY or INTELLIGENCE SUMMARY.

Army Form C. 2118.

of 30th (Northumbrian) Cyclist Company

(Erase heading not required.)

RE. MAPS 1/40,000

Hour, Date, Place	Summary of Events and Information	Remarks and references to Appendices
June 1st to June 3rd	The Company rested in A. Camp H.q.a. (Sheet 28)	
June 6th	The Company reconnoitred roads to report to 50th Division a. clean.	
June 4th to June 23rd Farm in G.26.a (Sheet 28)	Billets in a farm in G.26.a (Sheet 28). During this period the Company was employed in digging in reserve trenches for the 50th Div. Signal Company. 1st line, buried 2 foot 6 inches deep, ran from the ECOLE DE BEIM in H.24.a. (Sheet 28), a distance of about 3000 yards to KRUISSTRAAT. 2nd line, buried 2 foot 6 inches deep, ran from the ECOLE DE BEIM FAISANCE DE LE ETAT. I.9.c.5.o. (Sheet 28) to KRUISSTRAAT FAISANCE DE LE ETAT in I.9.c.5.o (Sheet 28) to NORTH corner of ETANG DE ZILLEBEKE in I.15.d. (Sheet 28), a distance of about 1000 yards.	
June 23rd	The Company exchanged billets with the 1st Lincolnshire Cyclist Company who were then at ST. JANS CAPEL in R.36.C. (Sheet 27.)	A Myrael Capt O.C. 30th Divisional Cyclist Company

Army Form C. 2118.

WAR DIARY of 50th (North'n) Divisional Signal Company.
INTELLIGENCE SUMMARY.
(Erase heading not required.) REMAPS 1/40,000

Instructions regarding War Diaries and Intelligence Summaries are contained in F.S. Regs., Part II. and the Staff Manual respectively. Title pages will be prepared in manuscript.

Hour, Date, Place	Summary of Events and Information	Remarks and references to Appendices
June 24th ST JANS CAPEL	A working party was out from the Company to work on the G.H.Q. trenches at ZILLEBEKE — I.22.b and I.22.d (Sheet 28) Casualties of the above working party, 2 Other Ranks wounded.	
June 25th to June 30th ST JANS CAPEL	During the above the Company found working parties to strengthen the G.H.Q. line in N.27.d, N.33.b and N.33.d. (Sheet 28).	A N Grace Capt O.C. 50th Divl. Sigt. Coy.

Army Form C. 2118.

WAR DIARY of the 1/4th (Northern) Divisional Cyclist Company
INTELLIGENCE SUMMARY.
(Erase heading not required.)   RE MAPS 1/30000

Instructions regarding War Diaries and Intelligence Summaries are contained in F.S. Regs., Part II. and the Staff Manual respectively. Title pages will be prepared in manuscript.

Hour, Date, Place	Summary of Events and Information	Remarks and references to Appendices
July 1st to July 19th 1915 ST. JANS CAPEL	During this period the Company was employed in digging in over for the Signal Company 28th Division. The approximate areas were these:— 1. From T.6.d.5.5 to T.6.a.5.5. (Sheet 28) a distance of about 600yds. 2. " N.33.q.3.4. to T.b.a.3.5. (Sheet 28) a distance of about 250 yds 3. " T.5.a.7.9. to T.5.b.8.10.8. (Sheet 28) a distance of about 600 yds 4. " N.27.a.1.9. to N.27.c.9.8. (Sheet 28) a distance of about 550 yds 5. " N.33.d.3.1. to N.34.c.2.6. (Sheet 28) a distance of about 600 yds 6. " N.36.c.5.3 to T.6.a.5.3 (Sheet 28) a distance of about 500 yds All the above were dug 2 feet 6 inches deep. Casualties during the above work — Pte. The Rank wounded	4 Cyclists Yorkshire Hussars enlisted in digging were 1 and 2
July 19th	The Company moved to ARMENTIERES and were billeted in	
July 19th ARMENTIERES	147, RUE SADI CARNOT. The Company found a carrying party for R.E. Jewellery Company.	ANGrace Capt. 1/6 30 4th Div. Cyclist Coy

WAR DIARY of 50th (Northumbrian) Division Cyclist Company

INTELLIGENCE SUMMARY

(Erase heading not required.) R.E. MAPS 1/40,000

Army Form C. 2118.

Hour, Date, Place	Summary of Events and Information	Remarks and references to Appendices
July 20 to July 31st ARMENTIERES	During this period the Company was employed as under:— (i) Fatigue parties & Guards at Divisional H.Q. (ii) Repaired Strong Points near ARMENTIERES in squares C.27 and J.1 & 2. (Sheet 36.) (iii) Reconnoitred the Divisional Area and handed over as guides.	A Myrace Capt O.C. 50th Div. Cyclist Coy.
Aug 6th ST. JANS CAPEL	2nd Lieut. R.W. PARKER reported for duty with the Company.	
Aug 17 ST. JANS CAPEL	1 Other Rank wounded whilst guarding Pr. with a MONT NOIR.	

WAR DIARY of 50th (North) Divisional **Cyclist Company**

or

INTELLIGENCE SUMMARY.

(Erase heading not required.)

Army Form C. 2118.

RE MAPS 1/40000

Hour, Date, Place	Summary of Events and Information	Remarks and references to Appendices
August ARMENTIERES	The Company carried out the undermentioned works:— (i) Dug communication trench from I.2.b.6.3. to I.3.a.7.3.0 when it cut with trench boards made by former owners of company. This trench was afterwards called LUNATIC LANE (ii) Dug communication trench from I.4.b.4.5. to I.4.b.5.4. (iii) Dug new wired hop sap in ca dugout from I.1.d.6.7.to I.9.b.6.3. (iv) Constructed loctice trenches & hut at Personal General School, which was started by the Cyclist Company. In addition to the above the Company supplied throughout the month guards & fatigues for Bde. H.Q. and several small working parties for the R.E. PARK.	A M Grace Capt O.C. 50th Divn Cyclist Coy

Army Form C. 2118.

WAR DIARY of 50th (North) Division Cyclist Company

INTELLIGENCE SUMMARY.
(Erase heading not required.) REMAPS 1/40000

Hour, Date, Place	Summary of Events and Information	Remarks and references to Appendices
August 13th ARMENTIERES	The undermentioned draft of reinforcements joined the Company. 27 other Ranks from the Northern Cyclist Batt. 14 other Ranks from the 2nd line North'n His. Cyclist Coy.	
August 20th ARMENTIERES	1 reinforcement joined the Company from the 2nd line North'n His. Cyclist Coy.	A M Grace Capt. O.C. 50th Div. Cyclist Coy.

WAR DIARY of 50th (North) Divisional Cyclist Company

INTELLIGENCE SUMMARY

Army Form C. 2118.

RE MAPS 1/40,000

Hour, Date, Place	Summary of Events and Information	Remarks and references to Appendices
September ARMENTIERES	During September 1915 the Company has:— (I.) Dug communication trench from I.3.b.6.5 to I.3.b.9.3 (Sheet 36) (II.) Buried wire from C.26.d.6.5 to I.2.b.9.7 (Sheet 36) (III.) Buried wire from C.27.d.8.8 to C.28.d.5.0 (Sheet 36) (IV.) Buried wire from C.27.c.8.7 to C.28.d.50 (Sheet 36) (V.) Supplied guides for troops who were working the area for the first time. (VI.) 30 men of the Company were employed at the Gravenstafel School. In addition to the above the Company supplied throughout the month guards, fatigues for Div. H.Q. and a number of working parties for the 50th Divisional R.E. PARK.	A Myrael Capt O.C. 50th Div. Cyclist Coy.

Army Form C. 2118.

WAR DIARY of 50th (North'n) Divisional Cyclist Coy
or
INTELLIGENCE SUMMARY.
(Erase heading not required.)

RE MAPS 1/40000

Hour, Date, Place	Summary of Events and Information	Remarks and references to Appendices
Left 4th ARMENTIERES	The Company was inspected by Major-General P.S. WILKINSON, C.B., C.M.G. commanding 50th (Northumbrian) Division.	
Left 7th ARMENTIERES	1 Other Rank wounded afterwards died of wounds.	
Left 13th ARMENTIERES	2nd LIEUT P.J. PHILLIPS & 2nd LIEUT H.M. STONE reported for duty	J M Wrack [?]
Left 25th ARMENTIERES	3 Other Ranks reported for duty from the 2nd Line (Northn) Div Cyclist Company	Capt P.C. 50th Div Cyclist Cy

Army Form C. 2118.

WAR DIARY of 50th (Northumbrian) Divisional Cyclist Company.
or
INTELLIGENCE SUMMARY.
(Erase heading not required.) RE MAPS 1/40000

Instructions regarding War Diaries and Intelligence Summaries are contained in F.S. Regs., Part II. and the Staff Manual respectively. Title pages will be prepared in manuscript.

Hour, Date, Place	Summary of Events and Information	Remarks and references to Appendices
October 5th ARMENTIERES	A working party of 1 Officer and 17 Mechanics were sent from the Company to the 2nd Bays Detachment at CLAIRMARAIS	
October 6th ARMENTIERES	1 Officer Rank returned to duty with the Company from the Northern Cyclist Batt.	
October 27th ARMENTIERES	1 Officer and 20 Other Ranks returned to the Company on an inspection by His Majesty the King. The Company during the month were employed as under:— (1) Guards & Fatigues at Divn H.Q. (2) Guarding 6 Bridges over the river LYS (3) Supply fatigues for the R.E. PARK (4) Repairing the Funds & Tramway Lots at the Divisional Grenade School.	A Myrard
October 23rd ARMENTIERES	1 Officer Rank reported for duty with the Company from the 3rd Line North umbrian Divisional Cyclist Company	A Myrard Capt ½ O.C. 50th Div. Cyclist Coy

Army Form C. 2118.

WAR DIARY
or
INTELLIGENCE SUMMARY.
(Erase heading not required.)

of 50 (Northumbrian) Divisional Signal Company.
RE MAPS 1/20,000

Instructions regarding War Diaries and Intelligence Summaries are contained in F.S. Regs., Part II and the Staff Manual respectively. Title pages will be prepared in manuscript.

Hour, Date, Place	Summary of Events and Information	Remarks and references to Appendices
November 1st to 11th ARMENTIERES	During this period the company was employed as under:- (i) Finding guards for the bridges over the L+S and Div. H.Q. (ii) Finding fatigue parties for the R.E.	
November 12 ARMENTIERES	The Company was relieved by the 21st Divisional Signal Company, and proceeded to MERRIS and was in three hours about 400 yards NORTH of MERRIS CHURCH	
November 12 to 30 MERRIS	During this period the Company trained in Signal work in connection with A + Q and Yorkshire Hussars.	
November 23rd MERRIS	The Company, together with the 150th Inf. Brigade and 4 Yorkshire Hussars, was inspected by General Sir Herbert E.O. Plumer K.C.B. commanding 2nd Army.	
November 18 ARMENTIERES	10th Rank wounded. This man was one of a party of men left in ARMENTIERES at the R.E. PARK where the Company moved to MERRIS.	A W Price Lieut. RE 50th (N) Div. Sig. Coy.

Army Form C. 2118.

WAR DIARY of 50th H.Q. (North) Divisional Cyclist Company.
or
INTELLIGENCE SUMMARY.
(Erase heading not required.) RE MAPS 1/40,000

Hour, Date, Place	Summary of Events and Information	Remarks and references to Appendices
Dec 1st to 16th MERRIS	The company continued cyclist training in camp and worked with "A" Sqd. Yorkshire Hussars.	
December 16th	The company changed billets with the 9th Divisional Cyclist	
December 16th to 31st WIPPENHOEK	Company who were at WIPPENHOEK in L.34.d (Sheet 27) During this period the company was employed as under:— 1 Officer 17 O.R. 2nd Army Woodcutting detachment 1 Officer 41 O.R. Road Control under A.P.M. 5th Corps 45 O.R. Road Control under A.P.M. 50th Division 70 O.R. Police under A.P.M. 5th Corps. 2 officers 300 O.R. Training as guides within the Division's Area 100 O.R. attached to 50th Divisional Ambulance 30 O.R. attached to 50th Division R.E. Park 4 O.R. attached to Pastel dumps.	

A Wyrall Capt
O.C. 50th Div Cyclist Coy

50th Division Cyclist Coy

Jan

Vol III

Army Form C. 2118.

WAR DIARY of 50th (Northumbrian) Divisional Cyclist Company
or
INTELLIGENCE SUMMARY.
(Erase heading not required.)

R.E. MAPS 1/40000

Instructions regarding War Diaries and Intelligence Summaries are contained in F.S. Regs., Part II. and the Staff Manual respectively. Title pages will be prepared in manuscript.

Hour, Date, Place	Summary of Events and Information	Remarks and references to Appendices
Jan 1st 1916 WIPPENHOEK	During the month the Company was employed as under :- 1 Officer 16 Other Ranks 2nd Army Woodcutting Company 1 Officer 41 Other Ranks Road Control under A.P.M. 5 Corps 45 Other Ranks Road Control under A.P.M. 50 Division 7 Other Ranks Police under A.P.M. 5th Corps 2 Officers 30 Other Ranks Training as guides within the Divisional Area 2 Other Ranks attached to Divisional R.E. Parks 3 Other Ranks attached to 50th Divisional Ordnance The remainder of the Company is employed on the construction of trackie trucks & put at the New Divisional Grenade School started by the Company at Wyncrestighe in L.33.d. (Sheet 27) D.E. 50th (North) 1 Other Rank is reported for duty with the Company forms the 2nd Army North'n Div. Cyclists Coy. Divisional Cyclist Coy	

Army Form C. 2118.

WAR DIARY of 50th North'n Division
Cyclist Company
or
INTELLIGENCE SUMMARY.
(Erase heading not required.)

Hour, Date, Place	Summary of Events and Information	Remarks and references to Appendices
Feb 1st 1916 WIPPENHOEK	During the month the Company was employed as under:- 1 Officer 16 Other Ranks 2 Army Headquarters Detachment 1 Officer 41 Other Ranks Road Control under A.P.M. 6 Corps 1 Officer 15 Other Ranks Road Control under A.P.M. 14 Corps 7 Other Ranks Police under A.P.M. 6 Corps 2 Officers 30 Other Ranks having as guides with the Divisional HQ 1 Officer 4 Other Ranks attached to Divisional R.E. Park 2 Other Ranks attached to 50th Divisional Ordnance Casualties Feb 19th 1916 1 Other Rank wounded Feb 19th 1916	AWyness Capt O.C. 50th Div. Cyclist Coy

Army Form C. 2118.

WAR DIARY of 50th (North'd) Divisional Cyclist Company
or
INTELLIGENCE SUMMARY.
(Erase heading not required.)

Instructions regarding War Diaries and Intelligence Summaries are contained in F.S. Regs., Part II. and the Staff Manual respectively. Title pages will be prepared in manuscript.

Hour, Date, Place	Summary of Events and Information	Remarks and references to Appendices

March 1st WIPPENHOEK — During the month the Company was employed as under:—

1 Officer 15 Other Ranks 2 Army forwarding detachment
1 Officer 29 Other Ranks Road Control under A.P.M. 5th Corps
19 Other Ranks Road Control under A.P.M. 50th Division
5 Other Ranks Police under A.P.M. 5th Corps
2 Officers 30 Other Ranks having no guide within the Divisional area

2 Other Ranks attached to Divisional R.E. Park
2 Other Ranks attached to 50 Divisional Ordnance

The Company was relieved by the 1st Canadian Divisional Cyclist Company. The 50 Divisional Cyclist Company took over the billets of the 2 Canadian Divisional Cavalry in M.16.C. central Sheet 28.

March 31 WIPPENHOEK

Army Form C. 2118.

WAR DIARY
or
INTELLIGENCE SUMMARY.
(Erase heading not required.)

Instructions regarding War Diaries and Intelligence Summaries are contained in F.S. Regs., Part II. and the Staff Manual respectively. Title pages will be prepared in manuscript.

Of 56th A/M Bgd Divisional Cyclist Company.

Hour, Date, Place	Summary of Events and Information	Remarks and references to Appendices
WESTOUTRE 11/4/16 to 25/4/16	The men of the Company were employed during this period as under:- 1 Officer 15 Other Ranks 2 Army Woodcutting Detachment. 1 Officer 72 Other Ranks Road Repaired and Trenches dug. A Bombers School was started by the Company.	
WESTOUTRE 25/4/16	The Company moved into billets in R.31.a.2.6. Sheet 27. on Handover of the Billets at WESTOUTRE to the 3rd Divisional Cyclist Company. During this period the Company have	
FLETRE 5/4/16 to 30/4/16	During the period 5 Other Ranks wounded while baking after storm.	
WESTOUTRE 6/4/16	5 Other Ranks wounded	

A Wyrack Capt
OC 50th Divisional Cyclist Company.

Army Form C. 2118.

WAR DIARY of 50th (North'n) Divisional Cyclist Company
or
INTELLIGENCE SUMMARY.
5 Corps
(Erase heading not required.)

Instructions regarding War Diaries and Intelligence Summaries are contained in F. S. Regs., Part II and the Staff Manual respectively. Title pages will be prepared in manuscript.

Hour, Date, Place	Summary of Events and Information	Remarks and references to Appendices
FLETRE 1/5/16 to 19/5/16	During this period the Company was in the rest area and trained in conjunction with "A" Sqdn Yorkshire Hussars.	
FLETRE 20/5/16	The 50th Divisional Cyclist Company was joined by the 24th Divisional Cyclist Company to form the V Corps Cyclist Battalion.	

A Ogracii Capt
O.C. 50th Divisional Cyclist Company

WAR DIARY of 1 Corps Cyclist Batt.

or

INTELLIGENCE SUMMARY.

(Erase heading not required.)

Army Form C. 2118.

Instructions regarding War Diaries and Intelligence Summaries are contained in F.S. Regs., Part II. and the Staff Manual respectively. Title pages will be prepared in manuscript.

Hour, Date, Place	Summary of Events and Information	Remarks and references to Appendices
21/5/16 FLETRE	The Batt moved the KEMMEL and took over there SECTORS of the DEFENCES namely VANCOUVER, WINNIPEG and TORONTO. The MONTREAL SECTOR was occupied by one squadron of the V Corps Mtd Troops and the O.C. V Corps Mtd Troops was in command of Hg DEFENCES.	
22/5/16 to 31/5/16 KEMMEL	The Battalion remained in KEMMEL DEFENCES during this period and worked on the Defences under the direction of OC V Corps Mtd Troops.	A Nyncu Major OC V Corps Cyclist Batt. OC V Corps Cyclist Batt.

www.ingramcontent.com/pod-product-compliance
Lightning Source LLC
Chambersburg PA
CBHW081505160426
43193CB00014B/2597